Alloa T

And the Erskines of Mar

Clackmannanshire Field Studies Society and Friends of Alloa Tower

Published by Clackmannanshire Field Studies Society and Friends of Alloa Tower
Marshill House, Alloa. Distributed by Forth Naturalist and Historian, University of Stirling.

First published 1973, by Clackmannanshire Field Studies Society - D.M. Dickie, K.J.H. Mackay
and E.K. Kennedy
Reprinted 1978
Revised 1987, by E.K. Roy (nee Kennedy), K.J.H. Mackay and L. Corbett.
Produced in co-operation with the Forth Naturalist and Historian, University of Stirling.
Revised edition 1996 by A.S. Bailey, K.J.H. Mackay, E.K. Roy, L. Corbett and I.G. Stewart.
This 3rd edition produced with the additional co-operation of the Friends of Alloa Tower

Publication data is available from the British Library.
ISBN 0-903650-10-X

Front cover photo, Alloa Tower from the West - Andrew Conoboy
Back cover photo, Coat of Arms of the Earl of Mar and Kellie.
Mosaic in roadway leading to Tower K.J.H. Mackay
Camera ready production, Alan Wilson

Printed in 'Lydian' BT true type on 100gsm environmentally friendly paper.
Printed by ATPRINT, Glenrothes.

Foreword

Alloa Tower is the oldest building in Alloa. It is one of the largest tower houses in Scotland and is of national importance, because of the seventeenth century alterations and the survival of the mediaeval roof.

After their arrival in Alloa around 1360, the Erskine family set about establishing a fortified home. The craftsmanship, design and materials used have been combined in a magnificent structure that not only survives today but also looks forward to serving the community as a special venue and as a visitor centre. I hope you will enjoy discovering Alloa Tower as much as I have done.

Jamie Erskine
14th Earl of Mar and Kellie

Introduction

"Unfortunately Alloa Tower has been allowed to fall into a state of severe decay, so it has not been accessible to the public, and it has had comparatively minor treatment in histories and guides. . .

"For centuries Alloa Tower has played a significant role in the history of Scotland. When the Tower was last open to the public (1973), the fabric could have been fully and usefully restored at relatively small expense; now unless extensive roof repairs are urgently put in hand very rapid deterioration will result. It is hoped that the importance of Alloa Tower will be officially recognised and action taken to restore this long neglected monument."

These rather sombre words concluded the 1987 edition of this book. At the time there appeared to be little hope for Alloa Tower, but within two years a massive restoration project was underway. The exterior of the building was made weathertight and completely re-pointed using authentic slaked lime mortar. The mediaeval oak roof was meticulously repaired, retaining as much of the original as possible. Outside, a year-long archaeological excavation of the remains of the 18th century house adjoining the Tower heralded the beginning of a landscaping programme of the area with new paths, planting and lighting. At the same time, the nearby 19th century stable block was converted for housing. At the time of writing (1995) work has begun on the internal restoration and conversion of the Tower into an historical interpretation centre with space for public use.

All the physical investigations and archaeological and historical research that these projects entailed brought to light much interesting new information about the history and structure of Alloa Tower. It was therefore decided to produce another edition of this book incorporating the new information, to help celebrate the Tower's re-birth. We hope you find it both interesting and enjoyable, and that it enhances your visit to Alloa Tower.

The Siting of Alloa Tower

From the watershed of Ben Lomond and Ben More, far to the west of Stirling, the River Forth and its tributaries flow eastward across the narrow waist of Scotland. From Aberfoyle to Stirling, meandering through a series of wide peat mosses, these waterways formed in past times an almost impenetrable barrier to the movement of early armies. Eastward from Kincardine-on-Forth, the widening estuary also proved a barrier to north-south movement.

However, the ten mile stretch of carse land and tidal river between Stirling and Kincardine is more accessible, and has played a vital part in the history of Scotland. From the early 13th century until the early 19th century, the river was readily crossed by several fords and ferries. Fortified structures guarded these "weak" points: Stirling castle defended Stirling Bridge; the ford at Manor was overlooked by Manor Castle; Alloa Tower did double duty guarding the ford and ferry at Alloa, and the ferries at Clackmannan and Higgins Neuk were watched over by Clackmannan and Tulliallan Castles.

Figure 1   Erskine crest.
Motto - "Je Pense Plus"(I Think More)

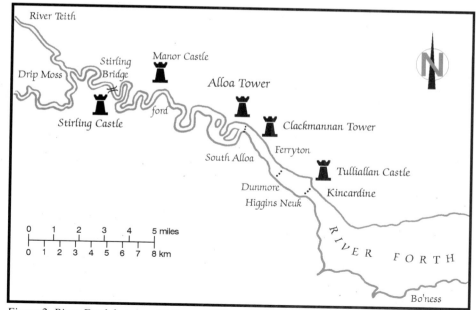

Figure 2   River Forth between Stirling and Kincardine, showing location of river crossings and fortifications.

Historical Background to the Erskine Family in Alloa

Since the 14th century the land on which Alloa Tower stands has been in the hands of the Erskine family. They originated from the parish of that name in the county of Renfrew. Though the barony does not appear among the lands granted by Malcolm IV to Walter, High Steward of Scotland, it is probable that the Erskines were native owners and became vassals of the Stewarts.

The first recorded mention of the name of Erskine is as a witness to a charter of Paisley Abbey in 1226. During the 14th century the Erskines gained in importance and influence. Sir Robert de Ereskyn rose to high position and added greatly to the family possessions. In 1368 the royal lands of Alloa were exchanged by David II for the Erskine lands of Strathgartney on Loch Katrine side. This grant included

> "the lands of Auleway (Alloa) and Galbardstoun (Gaberston) with the isle called the isle of Clackmannan and that part of the park of Clackmannan which adjoins the lands of Galbardstoun on the West side of the Water of the Little Devon, as that water runs within the shire of Clackmannan,..... also the new park beside Stirling and the land called Brenhalgh with pertinents within the forest of Clackmannan with the grazing of that whole forest.... Moreover, remembering the thankful service and careful labour unceasingly given by his said confederate, he grants to him the lands of Ferrytoun, the meadow of Clackmannan and a part of the park on the East side of the Water of Little Devon, to be held for the payment of half the service of a knight and three suits of court at the Sheriff court of Clackmannan."

Though there is a reference to the "manor house of Alloa" in 1448, the first surviving mention of the Tower itself is in a charter of 1495. Until modern times these lands have remained in the hands of Sir Robert's descendants.

Sir Robert, who was Captain of Stirling Castle, rose to the position of High Chamberlain of Scotland and served as Ambassador to the courts of France, England and the Papal See. On the death of David II, Sir Robert supported the claim of the High Stewards of Scotland to the throne, forging a link with the Stewart family which was to last for generations.

Figure 3 Arms of Erskine Earls of Mar.

2

Earldom of Mar – Origin lost in remote Antiquity

I. Ancient Pictish Line

1,2 & 3	4, 5 & 6	7, 8 & 9	10 & 11	12	13
1. Murtachus, maormor of Mar, 1065, styled 1st earl. 2. Gratnach, his son second earl, 1114. 3. Morgundus, son of Gratnach, reign of David I.	4. Gillocher, son of Morgundus. 5. Morgund, son of Gillocher, 1171 Reign of William the Lion. 6. Gilbert, son of Morgund.	7. Gilchrist, 8. Duncan, brothers of Gilbert. Earl Duncan died before 1234. 9. William, son of Duncan. One of the Regents of Scotland. 1258. Died 1270.	10. Donald, William's son, died 1294. His elder daughter, Isabella, queen of Robert I 11. Gratney, Donald's son. M. Christian Bruce, sister of Robert I.	12. Donald, son of Gratney. Regent of Scotland. August 2nd, 1332. Slain at Dupplin Moor, August 12th, 1332.	13. Thomas, Donald's son. Great chamberlain of Scotland, 1358. Died 1377, without male issue. *Direct male line extinct.*

II. Earls in right of Marriage with, or by Descent from, Female Heirs.

III. Abeyance of Hereditary Line

1 & 2	3	4	1	2	3
1. William, 1st earl of Douglas, husband of Countess Isabel, daughter of earl 2. James their son, earl of Douglas and Mar. Slain at Otterburn, 1388. No male issue.	3. Sir Malcolm Drummond, first husband of Countess Isabella, sister of earl James. died without issue, 1403.	4. Alexander Stewart, natural son of earl of Buchan, Wolf of Badenoch, second husband of Countess Isabella, 1404. Died without legitimate issue, 1435.	Title adjudged to the crown, 1457. 1. John, third son of James II. Put to death 1479. Cochrane, titular earl, favourite of James III. Hanged over Lauder Bridge 1482.	2. Alexander Stewart, duke of Ross, third son of James III. Created 2nd March, 1486. date of death unknown.	3. Lord James Stewart, earl of Moray, natural brother of Queen Mary. Created 1562. Preferred title of Moray. Regent 1567. Assasinated 1570.

IV. Line of Erskine – (I. Title unacknowledged).

1. (Title assumed.)		2. (Not assumed.)	3. (Not assumed.)	4. (Not assumed.)	5. (Not assumed.)
1. Sir Robert Erskine of Erskine, only son of Sir Thomas Erskine and Lady Janet Keith,	great grand-daughter of Gratney, 11th earl. Assumed title 1435. died 1452 Title adjudged to the crown 1457.	2. Thomas, 1st Lord Erskine, son of Sir Robert. Died before December, 1494.	3. Alexander second Lord Erskine, his son. Died before 17th June, 1510.	4. Robert third Lord Erskine, son of Alexander, second Lord. Slain at Flodden, 1513.	5. John fourth Lord Erskine, son of Robert, third Lord. Died 1552.

IV. Line of Erskine – (II. Title recognised).

1. (Properly 6.)	2. (Properly 7.)	3. (Properly 8.)	4. (Properly 9.)	5. (Properly 10.)	6. (Properly 11.)
1. John, fifth Lord Erskine, son of fourth lord. First acknowledged earl of "Erskine family," 1565. Regent 1571. Died 1572.	2. John his son. Born about 1558. Lord High Treasurer of Scotland. Died 1634.	3. John, Lord High Treasurer's son. Died 1654.	4. John, his elder son. Died 1668	5. Charles, last earl's elder son. Died 1689.	6. John, son of Earl Charles. Leader of rebellion, 1715. Estates and titles forfeited. Died 1732.

Title under attainder.

7. (Properly 12.)	8. (Properly 13.)
12. Thomas, Lord Erskine, son of 11th earl. Died 1766.	13. Jas. Erkine, kt. mar. of Scotland. son of Hon. James Erskine Lord Grange brother of 11th earl. M. Frances, only daughter of 11th earl. Died 1784.

Line of Erskine continued.

JE PENSE PLUS

Attainder reversed.

9. (Styled 14.)	10. (Styled 15.)
9. John Francis Erskine, son of James, knight marischal. Attainer reversed in his favour 17th June, 1824. Died 1825.	10. John Thomas, his son. Born 1772. Died 1828.

11. (Styled 16.)
11. John Francis Miller, 33rd in descent from Murtachus maormor of Mar.	Born 1795. Succeeded as earl of Kellie, 1829. Premier earl. viscount and baron of Scotland.

Figure 4 Earldom of Mar. Original drawn in the 19th century to establish the Erskine claim to the Earldom. From *'Scottish Nation'* (Anderson 1863)

ARMORIAL BEARINGS OF MAR AND KELLIE.

Quarterings; - 1 and 5 for earldom of Mar 2, 4 & 6 for Erskine, and 3 for earldom of Kellie.

Claim to the Earldom of Mar

Sir Thomas Erskine succeeded his father Sir Robert about 1387. His second wife, Janet Keith, widow of Sir David Barclay of Brechin, could trace her lineage back to Gratney Earl of Mar in the time of King Robert the Bruce. This relationship was the basis for the Erskine claim to the Earldom of Mar, though about 200 years were to pass before the claim was ratified.

Sir Robert, son of Sir Thomas, was the first to be dignified with the title of Lord Erskine; this was in 1438 during the reign of James II. The relationship seems to have become a little shaky a few years later, and Alloa Tower was seized by the crown during a land dispute. It was returned by James III in 1467.

Later Erskines continued to enjoy the favour of monarchs and performed their duties nobly. Alloa remained their home for the next three centuries. Alexander, 3rd Lord Erskine, had the charge of James IV when he was prince of Scotland. John, 5th Lord Erskine, succeeded to the barony after the death of his father at Flodden in 1513. He was Governor of both Stirling and Edinburgh Castles and was one of the guardians of James V during his minority (1513-28). He was also placed in charge of James Stewart, later Earl of Moray, the illegitimate son of James V and Margaret Erskine, sister to Sir John.

He was one of the guardians of Mary Queen of Scots during her minority. On the death of James V at Falkland in 1542, his daughter Mary, only a few days old, became Queen. On the 22nd of July 1543, seven months after the death of her father, Mary was brought to Stirling Castle, and crowned Queen in the Chapel Royal there on 9th September. She was then nine months old. Until 1548 she remained in the care of Lord Erskine at Stirling Castle and perhaps at his home in Alloa, except for short periods when her safety was threatened by the English army, during the time known as the "Rough Wooing". Henry VIII sought to unite Scotland and England by securing the consent of the Scottish leaders to a marriage of their Queen with Prince Edward, heir to the English throne. When the Scots rejected the suggestion, he sent an army north, hence Mary was taken for safety to Dunkeld in 1544; and in 1547 after further incursions by the English she was moved to the island Priory of Inchmahome on the Lake of Menteith, which was also held by the Erskine family. In the same year, Robert, eldest son of Sir John Erskine, was killed at the battle of Pinkie. In 1548 Mary was installed in Dumbarton Castle, whence she sailed for France accompanied by her guardian Lord Erskine to be betrothed and later married to the Dauphin. The Dauphin became King Francois II in 1559 making Mary Queen of France, as well as Scotland. He died tragically soon in 1560.

Subsequent events were to show that Mary was grateful to her protectors the Erskine family. On the 19th of August 1561, Mary, Queen of Scots disembarked at Leith on her return from France. John, 6th Lord Erskine, was a member of her Privy Council. On 23 January 1565, Mary granted him the Earldom of Mar "in free earldom, fee and heritage." She recognised Lord Erskine's hereditary right, and was moved by gratitude to restore his heirs to their just inheritance.

Origins of Erskine Earldoms of Mar & Kellie

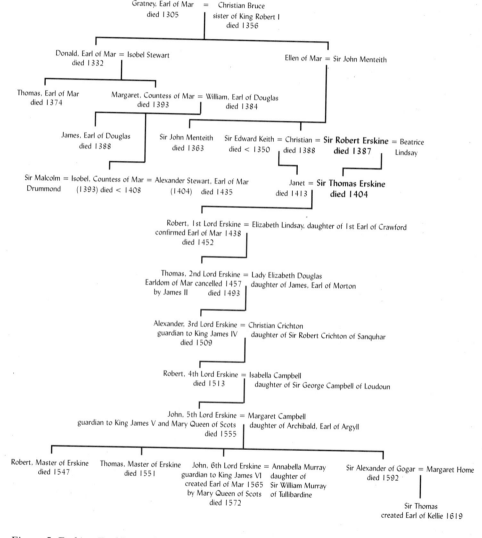

Figure 5 Erskine Earldoms of Mar and Kellie. Based on 'Scots Peerage' (1908)

5

Figure 6 Mary Queen of Scots.
by a follower of Clouet.

Under Mar's captaincy of Stirling Castle, Mary met and fell in love with Darnley, who was ill with measles in the castle at the time. They married in the same year, 1565. Their union was unhappy almost from the start and they separated after six months. Darnley soon became jealous of Mary's favoured Italian secretary David Rizzio, and on 9th March 1566 he formed one of the band of armed men who broke into the Queen's private apartments in Holyrood Palace, seized Rizzio and murdered him. Arthur Erskine of Blackgrange, brother of John the 6th Lord Erskine, is said to have been Mary's favourite equerry and was in attendance on her on the night of the murder.

Mary's son, Prince James, was born on the 19th June 1566, and the Queen, in poor health, went to Newhaven from Holyrood for a change of air. On the 27th June she sailed up the Forth to Alloa Tower into the care of the Earl of Mar, where she felt that she and her son would be secure. Darnley, seeking reconciliation, galloped round by Stirling and demanded to see her. He is supposed to have spent the night at Alloa, but he failed to see the Queen. The cradle and chair in which Mary reputedly nursed her son still belong to the Erskine family, and are now in the care of the National Museum of Scotland. It is odd that Mary is so famously associated with Stirling, Inchmahome and Linlithgow, but few people know of her connections with Alloa.

Prince James was placed under the protection and tutelage of the Earl of Mar to be "nursit and upbrocht". Like his mother before him, he lived his early life in the precincts of Stirling and perhaps Alloa, and his protector guarded him through the troublesome times of the first two Regents, the Earls of Moray and Lennox. After the murder of Lennox, the Earl of Mar himself became Regent, a post he held from September 1571 until his death on 28th October 1572.

Figure 7 The first Earl of Mar

6

There is a legend that Mary's son actually died soon after birth and that the future James VI was in fact a son of the Earl of Mar, substituted for the dead prince on the instructions of Queen Mary. This tradition was supposedly supported by the finding in 1830 of the body of an infant walled up in Edinburgh Castle, and portraits of the 2nd Earl of Mar and James VI were said to have shown an uncanny similarity. However, it is possible to trace the story to an over-romantic antiquarian of the late 19th century.

Figure 8 Mar highchair and cradle

On the death of Regent Mar, his son John, now 2nd Earl of Mar, was placed with James VI under the tutelage of George Buchanan and they were educated together at Stirling and Alloa.

Figure 9 James VI (left) and 2nd Earl of Mar. (right)

The Doom of Mar

Reputedly from the period around 1571 when the first Earl became Regent, a prophecy concerning the Erskine family has been handed down. Called "The Doom of Mar", it was attributed by some to the last Abbot of Cambuskenneth, and by others to the Earl's own bard.

1. *"Proud chief of Mar, thou shalt be raised still higher, until thou sittest in place of the King.*

2. *Thou shalt rule and destroy, and thy work shall be called after thy name; but thy work shall be the emblem of thy house, and shall teach mankind that he who cruelly and haughtily raiseth himself upon the ruins of the holy cannot prosper. Thy work shall be cursed and shall never be finished.*

3. *But thou shalt have riches and greatness, and be true to thy sovereign, and shall raise his banner in the field of blood.*

4. *Then, when thou seemest to be highest, when thy power is mightiest, then shall come thy fall. Low shall be thy head amongst the nobles of thy people. Deep shall be the moan among the children of dool. Thy lands shall be given to a stranger, and thy titles shall lie amongst the dead.*

5. *The branch that springs from thee shall see his dwelling burnt, in which a king was nursed, his wife a sacrifice in that same flame; his children numerous but of little honour; and three born and grown who shall never see the light.*

6. *Yet shall thine ancient tower stand; for the brave and true cannot be wholly forsaken. Thy proud head and daggered hand must dree thy weird until horses shall be stabled in thy hall, and a weaver shall throw his shuttle in thy chamber of state.*

7. *Thine ancient tower—a woman's dower—shall be a ruin and a beacon until an ash sapling shall spring from its topmost stone. Then shall thy sorrows be ended and the sunshine of Royalty shall beam upon thee once more. Thine honour shall be restored; and the kiss of peace shall be given to thy Countess, though she seek it not, and the days of peace shall return to thee and thine.*

8. *The line of Mar shall be broken, but not until its honours are doubled, and its doom is ended."*

The earliest reference we have found so far to this Doom dates from 1850, so we must be cautious in accepting it at face value. However, a comparison of this "prophecy" with the history of the Mar family makes interesting reading. Each part of the Doom contains elements of truth, but these must be examined in their historical contexts to determine their validity.

1. Becoming Regent in 1571, the 1st Earl sat "in place of the king."

2. In 1562, after the Reformation, he had acquired the Abbey of Cambuskenneth; popular tradition maintains that he ordered its destruction, in order to use the stones to build a mansion, Mar's Lodging, overlooking Stirling's market-place. It did not acquire the title "Mar's Wark" until 1732, when it was leased to the Town Council as the local work-house, and it suffered damage in 1746 during the siege of Stirling Castle by Bonnie Prince Charlie. The Doom refers to it as "thy work" throughout, suggests it represents "the ruins of the holy", and claims that it "shall never be finished." These aspects do not bear historical scrutiny. Mar's Lodging was in fact completed by 1572 to an elaborate design outstanding in Scottish town architecture and certainly not a building of patchwork made from the spoil of an old Abbey. Only some half-dozen stones appear to have been re-used from older structures. The building was lived in by the Earl and his descendants for more than a century. It even housed King James VI and his Queen in December 1593, while the Castle was being prepared for their reception. It is shown in one of the drawings in Slezer's *Theatrum Scotiae* of 1693 (Fig. 10), while Sir Robert Sibbald's description of Stirling, in the same work, states "Mar has a stately house of hewn stone of curious architecture. . .(which) adds much to the beauty of the town." The fact that this part of the Doom enshrines erroneous elements suggests that it was in fact written later and included odd legends which had grown up in the interim.

3. The Erskine family prospered. Successive Earls of Mar had honours showered on them— Governor of Edinburgh and Stirling Castles, Guardian of the Royal children, Ambassador to England, High Treasurer of Scotland. John, the 6th Earl, became Secretary of State for Scotland to the last of the Stuart sovereigns, Queen Anne. "Riches and greatness", indeed! However, Mar fell out of favour with Queen Anne's successor, George I, and became a leader in the Jacobite cause which aimed to restore the Stuarts to the throne. He led the ill-fated 1715 Rising and "raised his sovereign's banner in the field of blood" at the Battle of Sheriffmuir.

4. After the collapse of the Rising, he and the other leaders fled to exile in France. His lands were forfeited and his title extinguished. He died at Aix-la-Chapelle in May 1732. His lands were not "given to a stranger" but were purchased from the Crown by his brother Lord Grange, who was—at least outwardly—a loyal Hanoverian. Grange held the estate in trust for Mar's son, Thomas. However, the family title did, for a century, "lie amongst the dead."

5. The Doom then forecasts a fire and a resulting death at Alloa House "in which a king was nursed," which could refer to any of the infants James IV, V, VI or Charles I. It is a fact that in 1800 a fire destroyed the house, but because of prompt action by the local people, who built barricades of turf from the lawn, the Tower was saved. It is however incorrect to say that Mrs. Erskine died in the fire. Her death is recorded as having occurred two years earlier. The reference to "three born and grown who shall never see the light" is accurate: John Francis Erskine and his wife had a family of eight children, of whom three were born blind.

6. The ancient Tower stood on, preserved from the fire. A few years later it is said that 50 horses of a cavalry troop based at Alloa were stabled there during an alarm of a French invasion, and in 1810 that Mar's "Chamber of State" was occupied by a weaver who practised his trade for a fortnight before being discovered and evicted.

7. The Tower, referred to as a woman's dower (possibly because Lady Frances Erskine inherited it from her brother Thomas), was observed in 1815 to have an ash sapling growing from its "topmost stones", a promising omen, according to the Doom. When George IV visited Scotland in 1822 he received John Francis Erskine: "the sunshine of royalty." In 1824 the titles were restored, as forecast. His son, John Francis Miller Erskine, and his wife met Queen Victoria in Stirling Castle in 1840; the Countess was unexpectedly kissed by the Queen as a sign of Royal favour, "though she sought it not."

8. The final paragraph foretells a break in the line, a doubling of the title and the end of the Doom. The title of Earl of Mar was restored to John Francis Erskine in 1824. His grandson, John Francis Miller Erskine also succeeded to the earldom of Kellie, in 1829. He died without issue in 1866, and the titles were divided. The Mar title went to his nephew, John F.E. Goodeve-Erskine, and the Kellie title passed to his cousin Walter Coningsby Erskine, and then to Walter's son Walter Henry Erskine. After a famous legal case, an Act of Parliament was passed in 1885 which re-established the Earldoms of Mar and Kellie with the family at Alloa. After a break of 200 years, the position of Keeper of Stirling Castle was also restored, this time by George V. The Doom does indeed appear to be ended.

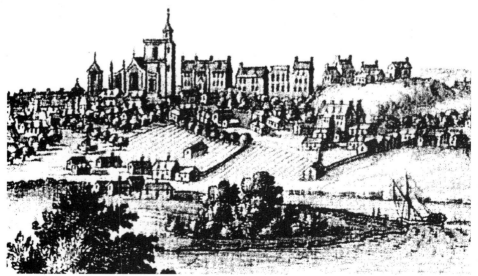

Figure 10   Drawing of Stirling by Captain John Slezer, circa 1693
showing Mar's Lodging, "a stately house", to the right of the church of the Holy Rude

Alloa's debt to the Erskines of Mar

To concentrate attention on the "Doom of Mar" is to ignore the positive contribution made by the Erskine family to the development of Alloa throughout the period of the "Doom". A sketch of Alloa by Captain John Slezer around 1693 shows an overcrowded group of buildings clustered around the tower. Yet by 1723 Alloa Tower and its surroundings were so transformed that Daniel Defoe could say of them,

"the Castle of Alloa is now so beautified, the buildings, and especially the gardens so completely modern that no appearance of a castle can be said to remain. . .The gardens are by much the finest in Scotland and not outdone by many in England. There is, in a word, everything that nature and art can do brought to perfection."

John, the 6th Earl, was not only one of the most powerful political figures in Scotland at the time, he was also a talented amateur architect and landscape designer, with a genuine concern for his people of Alloa. He was instrumental in improving Alloa, establishing a deep water port on the Forth, giving it an independent Customs House and so making it a centre for overseas trade. He encouraged the growth of supporting manufacture such as ropeworks, sailmaking, sawmills and shipbuilding, and he linked the thriving port to the expanding town by a spacious tree-lined avenue, then known as John Street and now represented by Broad Street and Lime Tree Walk. As a coal master he had to combat the problem of maintaining production; to improve the drainage of his mines he introduced more efficient water pumps; to operate these he constructed a reservoir at Gartmorn, fed by a lade from the Black Devon at Forestmill. The massive masonry dam which diverted the river into the lade still stands, impressive but neglected, as a monument to its creators. The Gartmorn reservoir was completed around 1713, and has had a value to Alloa which even the far-sighted Earl could hardly have guessed.

Figure 11   An extract from Slezer's drawing of Alloa. circa 1693. Alloa Tower is in the centre.

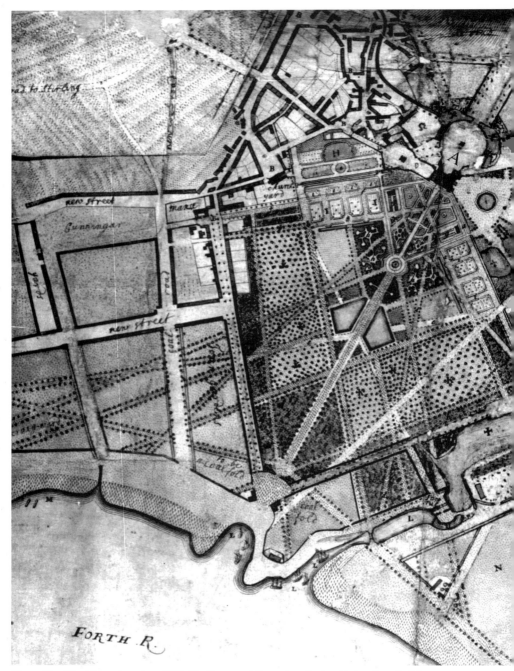

Figure 12. The Alloa estate circa 1720. The Tower and House is at A, the old church to the left

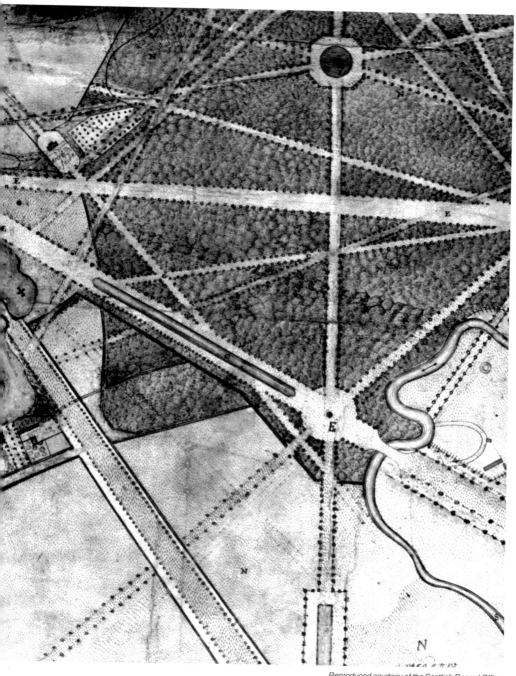

13

Mar also turned his talents closer to home, to his own house and gardens. As a young man he made the Grand Tour of Europe, taking a particular interest in architecture and gardens as he travelled. He is known to have made the acquaintance of the young James Gibbs at this time. Gibbs, born in Aberdeen in 1682, studied architecture in Holland and Italy. Eventually he was to become the arbiter of architectural fashion not just in Britain but as far afield as New England. In his younger days he wrote to the 6th Earl to ask for help obtaining a suitable post, and Mar, as Governor of Stirling Castle, arranged for him to be commissioned in the garrison there. Later Mar's repeated strong recommendations helped Gibbs become Sir Christopher Wren's successor as surveyor to the New Churches Commission in 1713. He designed the church of St. Martin - in - the Fields in London and Oxford's Radcliffe Camera.

Figure 13   6th Earl of Mar and son Thomas

We know that the Earl was having alterations made to Alloa House and gardens, and naturally would have consulted the architect he was currently recommending so highly. Gibbs is known at this time to have designed a Lodge or Summer house for the Earl on Comely Bank, on an avenue leading north-east from the Tower.

Gibbs and Mar remained close friends. It was to Gibbs that Mar wrote from exile in 1716 asking him to obtain possession of all his drawings. On his death in 1754, Gibbs bequeathed three houses, £1000 and all his plate to the Erskine children, Thomas and Frances.

Others who enjoyed the patronage of the 6th Earl, and contributed to the fame of the House and gardens of Alloa include Alexander Edwards, the right hand man of Sir William Bruce; Tobias Bauchop, Bruce's master mason and the founder of a famous dynasty of Alloa masons; Alexander McGill, the Earl's colleague and assistant, later a prominent architect in his own right; and William Boucher, the head gardener. Several of these continued to execute improvements to the House and gardens, on Mar's instructions, long after the Earl's departure.

Even after the 1715 Jacobite Rising, when his title and estates had been forfeited and he himself exiled to France, Mar's flow of bright ideas continued. Besides various alterations to Alloa House, he proposed the setting up of a glass works in Alloa, a 'New Town' for Edinburgh - very like the one which exists today - and the building of a Grand Canal across Scotland - a project which was, ironically, largely financed from the forfeited estates of the 1745 Rising!

By 1739 the majority of the forfeited Alloa estates (though not the Mar title) were returned to his son Thomas. He trebled the output of the coal mines, largely by substituting water and steam power for human labour in the raising of hewn coal and in the drainage of the mines. In his time, Alloa boasted some of the earliest waggon-ways in the country, with horse-powered operation, not merely increasing the coal exports from the harbour, but freeing his agricultural tenants from coal-hauling. Thomas also provided schools and encouraged the miners to take responsibility for managing their own affairs through their own Bailie Court.

His sister, Lady Frances, took the initiative in 1750 of establishing the Alloa Glass Works and ran this personally until 1767 when ownership was transferred to local merchants who expanded trade through the burgeoning brewing and distilling industries. From 1766 until 1777 she ran the estate and saw Alloa's prosperity grow. Wool spinning and weaving, tanning, pottery, iron founding and cabinet-making all contributed to the rise of Alloa's importance.

In 1777 she handed over control to her son, John Francis Erskine, who gave half a century of service to Alloa and its industries in a wide range of improvements, including roads, cornmills, a graving dock and an iron works. He introduced agricultural experts with the latest ideas - liming, manuring, crop rotation and two mechanical inventions, the metal plough and the threshing machine. In the mining industry his concern and that of his managers, Alexander

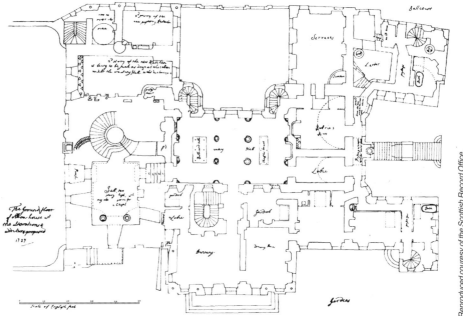

Figure 14   The ground floor of Alloa House with proposed alterations. The Tower with its curving Grand staircase is on the left, with the legend "Sall, two storeys high, Wch may also serve as a Chapel". Drawn by the 6th Earl in exile in 1727.

15

Bald and his son Robert, was for the welfare of his employees. Housing was improved, hygiene standards were laid down, education extended, a pension scheme introduced, a Friendly Society instituted, and women and children were no longer required to work underground. Coal production continued to increase, trebling during the course of his management. John Francis well deserved the eulogies of his biographer -"the late venerable Earl (the title was restored in 1824) endeared himself to his tenantry and his defendants by a life devoted to their happiness and an unremitting attention to the prosperity of Alloa."

John Francis Miller Erskine, who succeeded to the two titles of Mar and Kellie in 1828-29, made many improvements on the Alloa estate, including in 1834-38 a new mansion house to replace that destroyed by the fire of 1800, though on a different site. When young, he was a subaltern in the First Regiment of Foot Guards and was wounded at Waterloo. He died in 1866, without issue, and so the titles were divided. The Mar title went to his nephew, John F.E. Goodeve-Erskine, and the Kellie title to his cousin, Colonel Coningsby Erskine.

Colonel Coningsby Erskine had a distinguished military career in India and was awarded the title of Companion of the Bath. In the 1850s he employed local workmen and architects to alter and improve Alloa House. It was in fact largely rebuilt, and new stables (now known as Tower Square) were built elsewhere in the grounds. Gardens and environs were re-modelled, extensive shrubberies re-planted and the old Alloa Tower substantially repaired, with new concrete steps to the top so that visitors could climb up in safety. In the town, a new Episcopal church was built in Broad Street and ground was given free at Sunnyside for a hospital.

Colonel Coningsby Erskine died in 1872 in Cannes. He was succeeded by Walter Henry, an enthusiastic Freemason and Grand Master Mason of Scotland from 1881 to 1885. He kept the farm of Bowhouse in his own hands and took a personal interest in his tenants. In 1885, after a famous legal case, Walter Henry was declared to be Earl of Mar and Kellie, re-establishing the two titles with the family at Alloa. He died in 1888 at the early age of 48 and was succeeded by Walter John Francis Erskine, a Lieutenant in the Scots Guards. In 1892 he married Violet, daughter of the Earl of Shaftesbury and grand-daughter of the "Good Earl" who supported the cause of the poor and improved conditions in the mines, banning women and children from such work. At the birth of their first son in 1895 all the schoolchildren in Alloa and Sauchie (some 3000) had a grand fete in the grounds of Alloa House.

Walter John initiated the movement to commemorate the fallen of the South African War, and the resulting monument was unveiled in 1904 (it is now situated in a small park at Marshill). The Earl and Countess were accepted in Royal circles and frequently entertained exalted guests at Alloa House. The Earl held his title for 67 years, dying in 1955. He was succeeded by his grandson John, whose father and uncle had both died earlier. Alloa House was given up in 1959 and demolished, and much of the land is now under municipal housing. John also had a notable career in the Army, as a Major in the Scots Guards, and saw active service in World War II. He gave good service to the community and was assiduous in his duties as a local councillor and on other public bodies. After his death in 1993 he was succeeded by his son James, present 14th Earl of Mar and 16th Earl of Kellie.

The Uniqueness of Alloa Tower

Alloa Tower is a massive building, one of the largest surviving tower houses in Scotland. The walls are 11 feet thick and rise over 80 feet to the crenellated parapet. Because of the thickness of the walls it was possible to have a walkway all around the top, from which there is an extensive view in all directions. Like all tower houses, this one was designed to be a defensible retreat for the owner and his people.

However, Alloa Tower has many features that are unusual and indeed out of place on a building designed with defence in mind. Instead of a few small windows, irregularly placed wherever the internal arrangements demanded, it boasts four rows of large symmetrical openings, as well as false window recesses; instead of a first floor entrance with a removable stair, there is a wide ground floor doorway with an elaborately carved surround. Even the crenellations on the parapet may have been widened to improve the view. The interior, as we shall see, has been even more extensively altered.

When the Tower was built, probably in the late 14th century, defence was the most important consideration. However, over the years life became easier, and the later Erskines began to consider their comfort as well. A collection of outbuildings grew up around the Tower, including at least a stable and a kitchen tower. Major alterations were begun by Charles, 5th Earl, and triumphantly carried through by his son John. Some of the outbuildings were done away with, others were incorporated into a new, grand mansion on the south-east side of the Tower. The Tower itself became a wing of the house, with numerous passages connecting the two structures, and the exterior altered to bring its style more into line with the 'modern' house. The enlarged windows brought more light through the thick stone walls and into the Tower, and the false recesses, when painted with imitation glazing bars, gave a symmetrical appearance. Alloa Tower became an 18th century building in a mediaeval shell.

Figure 15 Watercolour of Alloa Tower and House in 1780 by "A.B."

The 6th Earl of Mar, according to John Ramsay of Ochertyre, "had a great turn for architecture", and is supposed to have designed the original Blairdrummond House, built between 1715 and 1719. His papers and plans certainly contain a wealth of projected architectural drawings including some which carry the 'present' design of Alloa Tower a stage or two further. Ramsay observed that "the '15 Rebellion broke out ere his additions to Alloa House were finished."

The famous parterred gardens (Fig. 12) survived at least until 1750, when they appear on General Roy's Map of the area. By 1780 they had been 'modernised' to the simpler style of the period. The house was destroyed by fire in 1800, except for the north-east wing which survived until the 1970s as a cottage.

GENERAL DESCRIPTION
EXTERIOR

NORTH WEST FACE

Alloa Tower faces north-west. The late afternoon sun brings out the warmth of its honey coloured sandstone. Its walls are built of rough stone arranged in regular rows of coursed rubble, which contrasts markedly with the well finished ashlar of the classical doorway. The handsome doorway included some personalised details: the Earl's crest in the centre above the door, a coronet surmounted by a hand holding an abbreviated sword and the arrogant motto "Je Pense Plus": (I Think More. - Fig. 1), and in the semi-circular fan light a lovely wrought iron screen including the letter 'M' for Mar. This ironwork was stolen, but a replacement has been installed.

This ornate doorway, so out of character with the strong, stark lines of the rest of the building, has sometimes been labelled a "Gibbs Surround", after a style associated with the 6th Earl's friend, James

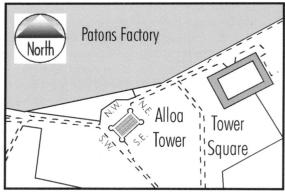

Figure 16   plan orienting tower

K.J.H. Mackay

Figure 17   original wrought iron fanlight

Gibbs. However, the discerning eye can see certain differences between the doorway of Alloa Tower and most Gibbs' surrounds. The Tower's door has more the style of Italian architecture of a century earlier, and is probably the design of the Earl himself. He had obviously observed and adopted several ideas from his Grand Tour, including doorways, grand staircases and domed ceilings. We should probably give him credit for developing a style of his own, more of which we may see when discussing the interior of the building.

The windows of the front are arranged with a forced symmetry, in four rows of five, with false recesses at the outer corners where real windows could not be cut because of the great thickness of the walls behind. The gap between the third and fourth rows is larger than the others because of the thickness of vaulting supporting the top floor. On the second floor, one can see the irregularity of the stonework where two original windows were filled in to allow two new openings to be cut in the correct position: no mean feat, given the thickness of the walls!

The three turrets on this face sit squarely along the line of the parapet on smoothly graded triple coursed corbels. The centre one was presumably designed to cover the central doorway. Each turret has modest crenellations and shot holes. The chimneys visible behind are of early 18th century date.

SOUTH WEST GABLE

The south-west side of the building was also given a face-lift in the 1700s to make it harmonise with the classical facade of the house. The rows of windows match the levels of those on the north-west front, though only the central one in each row is real. The window on the ground floor has clearly been used as a doorway at some time. The second floor window is slightly wider than standard, though not, apparently, enough to upset the architect Earl. The small windows on the right were cut to admit light to the spiral staircase in the south corner of the Tower, which previously had only three vertical slits in the upper levels.

The parapet above is crow-stepped at each end but level and low for four or five yards in the centre.

SOUTH EAST FACE

Because so much of this side was obscured by the house (see Fig. 14), it received much less artistic alteration, though it has clearly been extensively modified. Above the 'roof raggles' where the sloping roofs of the house were linked

Figure 18   The Tower seen from the rear prior to 1994

to the Tower - and these show changes as well - three windows open into the upper floor, and one into the second floor chamber. A smaller window lights the passage from the spiral stair to the second floor room. Seven blocked doorways, some of them arched, indicate the connections between Tower and house at ground and first floor levels. It may be that one of the first floor openings is a remodelling of the original defensible entrance to the tower. On the right, at first floor level, is a small blocked window with sockets surrounding it as if for an iron grill.

Overhead, two turrets are visible, linked by battlements with four simple crenellations and three splayed gun loops. Two red sandstone chimneys can also be seen.

NORTH EAST GABLE

This face of the Tower has also been little modified. It sports three windows in an almost vertical line. The various roof raggles of the North East wing of the house can be seen. This was the only portion of Alloa House to survive the 1800 fire, and was used as an estate cottage. At some point it was enlarged and modified.

At parapet level, there is another deep crow-stepped crenellation between the corbel rounds. The left hand turret has a latrine built into it. Just below, a slit window illuminated the garderobe on the upper floor. The gable of the attic roof with its ball finial and chimney stack is readily seen from this angle. A single large downspout carries all the runoff from the roof.

Figure 19 Vertical section from the front showing the four floors

20

INTERIOR

GROUND FLOOR

Entering through the main doorway one of the blocked up entrances to the mansion lies immediately ahead. To the right was an 18th or 19th century wall, removed during renovations. There is also a handsome fireplace of 18th century date, with another arched doorway beyond it.

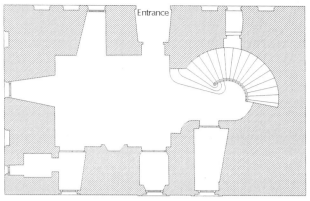

Figure 20   Ground floor plan

The great curving stair leading to the first floor may have been modelled on the Scala Granda in the Palazzo Farnese at Caparola. Originally the access to the first floor was probably by a more mundane and easily secured ladder through a trap door, with the first floor level occupying the whole width of the building.

Below the stair lies a vaulted cellar, unsuspected until work began to renovate the interior of the building. No entrance is visible, so it was probably sealed off when the stair was built.

FIRST FLOOR - GREAT HALL

Over the stairwell is a large dome, built of lath and plaster and suspended below the mediaeval vaulting of the upper floor. Above the stair is a minstrel's gallery, the balustrade ornamented with wrought iron work. In the south-west half of the first floor is some elaborate ornamental cornicing, possibly of 17th century date, as well as some of the 18th century painted decoration.

From here inside the building the visitor can see which are original mediaeval windows and which 18th century inserts. The original windows have round-arched tops, while the later ones have flat lintels, originally wood but in some cases since replaced in concrete for safety reasons.

When renovation work began a surprising discovery was made at this level: the Tower's

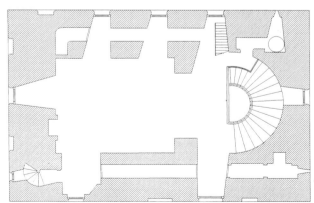

Figure 21   First floor plan.

21

original well, which occupied a chamber in the north corner of the building. It was filled in and blocked off during the 18th century renovations. It is a well-built circular shaft, running down through the thickness of the wall for some 22 feet into the bedrock below the Tower. The soft porous sandstone acted as a natural filter for water percolating into the well. A secure water source is always a prime consideration when designing a building to be defended, and the builders of Alloa Tower provided an excellent facility: any attacker would have had to tear the building down to cut off the water supply.

Standing in the Great Hall and facing the dome, you can see an arch framing the entrance. The sides continue down to the ground floor level, and this fact, in conjunction with details observed during the repair of the floor, seems to show that at one time this space was in fact open, leaving just a gallery around the first floor level. Certainly this is one of the features seen in the 6th Earl's plans. (The floor level of the well chamber is higher than the present floor, which may give us the original level.) Two corridors run through the thickness of the north-west and south-east walls; the southern one opens into a garderobe at its east end and leads west to the small spiral or turnpike stair which is the only access to the upper floors: another security feature.

SECOND FLOOR - CHARTER ROOM

This room now occupies only half the length of the Tower, the other half having been cut away to insert the dome. Two of the original rounded windows were retained, in the south-west and south-east sides (to your left beyond the fireplace and in the corner to your right as you enter the room), though their embrasures have been enlarged, while in the north-west side two new windows replaced an old one. (see p.25) The roof of this room is 'groin vaulted', that is, with two diagonal vaults crossing at right angles, there is a similar vault hidden by the dome. At some point the vaulting was hidden by a plain plaster ceiling, now removed. This has exposed fragments of the patterning of an early wall-paper.

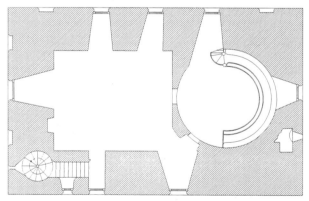

Figure 22   Second floor plan

22

Originally this room was probably the 'solar', the private living room for the lord and his family, situated high up for security, which also allowed larger windows and hence more light. Later, certainly by the 6th Earl's time, it became known as the library.

This grand room retains four original windows with stone seats and 'aumbreys' or cupboards cut into the walls. The other windows and the two fireplaces in the north wall are of later date. At the east end is a passage leading to the garderobe and the original mediaeval chimney. There was originally an attic floor above this one, and the remains of the stone corbels or brackets on which its floor rested can be seen high on the walls. The filled in doorway to the attic can be seen high in the north east wall.

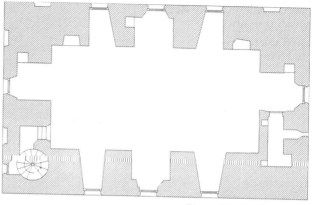

Figure 23 Top floor plan

One of the most remarkable features of Alloa Tower is the original mediaeval oak roof, one of very few of that age and quality surviving. It consists of 30 double couples of eight inch square timber. It is a massive construction, intended to support the weight of the sandstone slabs which originally roofed the Tower. These were replaced by the 6th Earl in slate, and that is how the roof was restored. The timbers themselves were replaced as necessary with pieces of modern oak from Loch Lomond side, retaining as much of the mediaeval timber as possible.

Figure 24 'Solar' prior to restoration showing the mediaeval roof

Bill Robertson

23

One of the 6th Earl's plans was to remove this roof and replace it with a flat lead tank filled with water. In it he would keep "fish and fowl", and from it would run the plumbing system for the house and fountains in the gardens. It was a feature which was installed in some noble houses in England, but, perhaps fortunately, Mar was never given the chance to execute it here. It might have saved the house when the fire began, but it would have meant the loss of the great mediaeval roof.

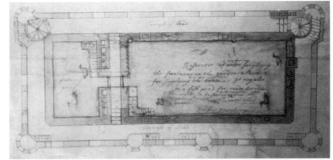

BATTLEMENTS

Figure 25 The 6th Earl's plan for the roof showing the water tank

The turnpike stair continues up to the roof, topped with a hollow capstone. At each corner of the tower and in the centre of the north-west wall the round corbelled bartizans allow an enhanced view in all directions: nine counties are visible from the roof of Alloa Tower- Perth, Kinross, Fife, Midlothian, West Lothian, Lanark, Stirling, Argyll and, of course, Clackmannan. On each gable is a mediaeval chimney stack, while those on the north-west side date to circa 1700 and those on the south east to later in the 18th century. In the north-east gable remnants of a blocked door to the vanished attic, replaced by a window, can be seen. The garderobe in the east corner has a lamp recess, and its roof was another lookout point.

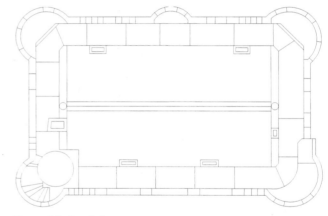

Figure 26 Roof plan

CONCLUSION

After the fire, Alloa Tower lost its function as a home which it had enjoyed for so many years. It was used for storage, for offices, for meeting rooms for some local organisations. Throughout this century its usefulness waned and it grew more dilapidated and unsafe. In 1973 it was briefly opened to the public as an Interpretive Centre from 2 to 13 July. With Lord Mar's blessing, and on the initiative of Clackmannanshire Field Studies Society, considerable voluntary endeavours cleaned up and opened the Tower. Displays were arranged which included an exhibition reflecting aspects of local history, an audio-visual programme, and the first edition of this booklet. The formal opening on 30 June by Lord and Lady Mar included music and dancing. 2800 visitors were recorded, some 200 people per day. On 26 October of the same year Princess Margaret's royal visit to Alloa included over an hour in the Tower which then remained open for a further two days.

On the 400th anniversary of the death of Mary Queen of Scots in 1987, the Tower was again opened to the public from 29th August to 19th September.

In 1987, Clackmannan District Council decided to act to save the Tower. In 1988 a charitable trust, the Alloa Tower Building Preservation Trust, was formed by the Council and the 13th Earl, the latter making the difficult decision to transfer ownership of the Tower and the remaining 5 acres of land surrounding it from the family to the Trust. In 1990 work commenced on the Tower and since then works have continued to revitalise this part of historic Alloa. Around twenty agencies have contributed, with major continuous funding from Clackmannan District Council, Historic Scotland, The Architectural Heritage Fund and the European Commission, with further support from Scottish Homes, Central Regional Council and Forth Valley Enterprise. The Trust's approach to the Alloa Tower and Old Town Enhancement Project has to date brought many national awards, most notably a 1994 UK Award for Planning Achievement from the Royal Town Planning Institute. In 1996, the National Trust for Scotland agreed to lease the management of Alloa Tower with the support of the new Clackmannanshire Council to allow it to open to the public. This is further evidence of the national importance of this once forgotten building, and a monument to the work of John the 6th Earl, who is now recognised as "a unique figure in British architectural history, an amateur architect of some distinction, with an able and fertile imagination" (Colwin, Bibliographical dictionary of British Architects 1995).

Selected Bibliography and Further Reading

Anderson, W. *Scottish Nation*. Fullarton, Edinburgh 1863

Brown, W. *Clackmannanshire guide to historical Sources*.
    Forth Naturalist and Historian 1980.

DeFoe, Daniel. *A tour through the whole Island of Great Britain*.... London 1769

Fleming, J.S., Gardner *Ancient Castles and Mansions of Stirling Nobility*.
    Paisley & London 1902.

Fraser, Antonia. *Mary Queen of Scots*. 1969.

Friedman, Terry. *James Gibbs*. Yale University Press 1984.

G.E.C. *Complete Peerage*. revised edition 1929. vol K. pp.190-206 for Earldom of Kellie;
    vol.M pp.398-433 for Earldom of Mar.

Harper, C.G. *Haunted Towers*. Palmer, London 1931

Historical Manuscripts Commission. *Report on Manuscripts preserved in Alloa House*.

Kirkdale Archeology. *Alloa Tower Archeological Recording*. 1996.

Little, Bryan. *James Gibb, Architect, Life and Work*. Batsford 1955

Macunn, Florence. *Life of Mary Stuart*. Nelson, 1907.

McGibbon and Ross. *Castellated and Domestic Architecture of Scotland*.
    Thin, Edinburgh 1971. vol. 1, pp.52-55.

Marsden, S. *Haunted Realm*. Guild, London 1986

Ramsay, John of Ochertyre. *Scotland and Scotsmen in the Eighteenth Century*.
    Blackwood 1888.

Ronald, J. *The Earl of Mar's Lodging*. Stirling 1905.

Royal Commission on the Ancient and Historical Monuments of Scotland.
    Inventory of Fife, Kinross and Clackmannan. HMSO 1933.

Scots Peerage. Douglas, Edinburgh 1908. vol.5, pp.590-636 on Erskines of Mar.

Smout, T.C. "The Erskines of Mar and the Development of Alloa."
    Scottish Studies vol. 7 1963 pp.57-64

Slezer, J. *Theatrum Scotia*. 1693.

Stewart, Margaret *Lord Mar's Plans*. M. Litt. thesis, University of Glasgow 1988.

Statistical Accounts of Scotland: Old 1791. vol. 8, p.594
New 1845. vol.8 pp.16-18,37-39,43.
Third 1966. ed. T. Crouther Gordon. vol. 18, pp.499-500, 511.

Tranter, N. *Fortified Houses in Scotland*. vol. 2, Thin, Edinburgh 1977.

Two local organisations have jointly contributed to the publication of this booklet: The Clackmannanshire Field Studies Society and the Friends of Alloa Tower. The CFSS was formed in 1970 to "stimulate interest in aspects of the local area, including past and present industries, and some local and natural history." Occasional courses, symposia or exhibitions have been run and it is associated with the Forth Naturalist and Historian's 'Man and the Landscape' annual symposium. There have been several research group projects including one which was published as a booklet 'Mines and Minerals of the Ochils'. Other publications include 'David Allan', 'Linn Mill', 'The Ochil Hills' and a twice yearly newsletter. Membership is open to anyone with an interest in or a desire to support the aims of the Society.

The Friends of Alloa Tower was formed in 1990 to provide a means for individuals to help support the restoration of the Tower. Money has been raised from membership fees, donations and fund raising events at the Tower and elsewhere. Several Open Days were organised during which hundreds of people visited the Tower. The Friends have hosted lectures and other events, as well as producing merchandise such as Alloa Tower mugs and tea towels. The Friends intend to continue an active role in the life of the Tower after its opening. Anyone who wishes to support the continuing success of this beautiful and important historic building is welcome to join.

Acknowledgements

The authors would like to thank Andrew Millar and the Alloa Tower Building Preservation Trust for help and support in the production of this book; Bob Heath, Terry Friedman and Margaret Stewart for architectural and historical advice; and Alan Wilson for all his work on the design layout and setting.

K.J.H. Mackay

K.J.H. Mackay

Figure 27   Some features of the restored Tower: the doorway, (top) the minstrel gallery and Grand Stair, (above left) the solar (right)

K.J.H. Mackay

28